FAST TRACK AN INDIVIDUALIZED COLLEGE PLAN FOR LIFE AFTER HIGH SCHOOL

ANDREA JONES-DAVIS

An Individualized College Plan for Life After High-School

Copyright © 2016 (Print) by Andrea Jones-Davis
Copyright © 2016 (Electronic) by Andrea Jones-Davis
Cover Design and Layout: Reshonda Perryman
Editor: Parthenia Fields

All rights reserved. No part of this publication may be reproduced, transmitted, stored in an information retrieval system, or used in any form or by any means, graphic, electronic, mechanical, photocopying, recording or otherwise, without the prior written permission of the publisher.

ORDERING INFORMATION

Workbooks are available for bulk purchases for educational use. Professional Development and Student Work Sessions are available upon request. For details, send request to The Next Chapter at *thenextchaptereditions@gmail.com* or contact Andrea Jones-Davis at 769-208-3558.

ISBN-10: 0-9979731-2-9
ISBN-13: 978-0-9979731-2-9

This book belongs to:

_____

ACADEMIC SCHOOL YEAR: _____

EXPECTED COLLEGE ATTENDANCE ACADEMIC SCHOOL YEAR: _____

MY SUPPORT TEAM:
(May include: parents, mentors, school counselors, alumni, etc.)

_____

_____

_____

_____

_____

FOREWORD

The time has come to find the best institution of higher learning that will meet your educational, social, and financial needs, and you have no idea where to begin.

The Next Chapter is an excellent workbook that will provide both parents and students with resources, strategies, and techniques to assist in making the student's next chapter in life a success.

The author of this workbook, Andrea Jones-Davis, has a strong educational background that has allowed her various opportunities to interact with students and parents who just did not know where to begin when it came to selecting the college best suited to their needs. Jones-Davis took these experiences and interactions with parents and students as well as her own children in order to construct a workbook that not only assists students in selecting a college/university of their choice but also determines if the selected university fits their budgets.

As a college professor who works with students daily, I found this workbook to be a dream come true. Time after time, parents and students call my office to ask several questions (e.g. Where should I go to school? Can we afford that university? What should be my major unit of study?). Jones-Davis has highlighted them in this workbook; now, the answers to these questions and more can be discovered right here at your fingertips in a workbook that will make selecting your best college a breeze.

What does your next chapter hold?

-Thea Williams-Black, *Ph.D.*

This workbook is dedicated to André & Coralyn.

My inspiration, motivation and encouragement. While I was busy teaching you many things about life and imparting knowledge, you couldn't imagine all that you were teaching me. I am who I am because of you. Thanks to both of you I am a better person. When my days aren't so bright, you are my sunshine. You have looked beyond my weaknesses and built up my strengths. I love you more!

Family, Friends & Supporters...To those who listened, cared, and believed in one more of my dreams, thank you! For all of the early mornings and late nights, thank you! For all of the encouragement and motivation, thank you! I expressed my idea and you helped make it happen. Thank you for guiding me in the right directions. Thank you for reminding me that giving up was not an option. Thank you for loving me and my family like your own. Thank you for all of your contributions that made The Next Chapter a real chapter in my life. I love you more!

PREFACE

Everyone's talking about college, and you have a ton of questions like...

Where will I attend?

How much will it cost?

Where do I begin?

Enter The Next Chapter: An Individualized College Plan for Life after High School.

While assisting my own children in preparing for and selecting institutions of higher learning, I recognized the need for others to have access to the tools that we used to select the best path for them. So, I decided to compile them into a workbook that clarifies and streamlines the-sometimes daunting and confusing-process of college selection into a step-by-step format.

Inside you will find tools created to help you choose the school that is right for you, information about college entrance exams, and how to best fund the upcoming adventure that is college. I have designed this workbook to answer all your questions about selecting a college and understanding their requirements.

Enough talk about the book. Let's get ready for *The Next Chapter*® of your life!

01 Introduction
02 *Let's Get Started!*
03 Tips

ABOUT YOU

05 Personal Profile
10 Career Goals
11 School Choice Profile
13 College Entrance Exams
15 Financial Sources
18 Scholarships

THE BREAKDOWN

21 Application Process
22 *Top 5* College/University Identities
23 The Starting 5/Classify
44 Compare
46 *Top 3* College/University Identities
62 Compare Again
63 *Top Choice!*

THE NEXT CHAPTER

65 Top Choice Breakdown
67 Learn the Area
69 Glossary
79 Appendix
104 Resources
105 About the Author

To the Student:

Welcome to *The Next Chapter*: An Individualized College Plan for Life After High School!

Making plans for life after high school can be really exciting as well as somewhat frightening. There are so many decisions to make and so many questions to answer. The Next Chapter workbook will serve as a guide to help you be well prepared for your future by developing an Individualized College Plan (ICP)*. Hopefully, this workbook will answer all of those questions you might have to make any decisions a little easier for you. Whether you choose public or private, community or online, vocational or technical college or university, this workbook will help you understand college terminology and the major factors when choosing a post-secondary educational institution. Use this workbook as a resource to list major factors such as location, size, cost, and academic quality of possible college choices, so you can better compare your options. As you venture through The Next Chapter, think carefully about any high school requirements that you may need to complete for graduation.

***REMEMBER**: Make this a fun adventure while moving full speed ahead into the next chapter of your life. Enjoy the experience!*

ICP *n.* an individualized plan developed by the student to assist with understanding collegiate terminology, educational options and determining factors when choosing a college.

To the Parents or Guardians:

All students should have a plan for life after high school. It is an exciting time! The Next Chapter workbook will serve as a guide to help your future graduate be better prepared to develop their Individualized College Plan (ICP).

ASK YOURSELF: *Is your student prepared to identify, analyze, evaluate, and finalize their college choices?*

Don't allow your student to choose a college based on brand name. Rather, help him or her choose a school that fits the individual needs of the student. After completing this book, prospective graduates will be able to understand college terminology, develop an Individualized College Plan (ICP), and address major factors concerning choosing a college. For optimal results, you should walk through this workbook with your student to help him or her understand the college preparation process.

***REMEMBER**: Make this a fun adventure while helping your child move forward to the next chapter of their lives.*

Are You ready?

Let's Get Started!

Now, you're ready to begin! Make sure you have set aside some uninterrupted time and gather the necessary items to complete your Individualized College Plan (ICP).

ITEMS YOU MAY NEED:
- Computer – Desktop, laptop or tablet
- Internet connection
- Current school transcript
- A parent/guardian
- Paper/pencil/pen
- School Counselor/Records Clerk
- Any college information (brochures, etc.)
- Available scholarship information

Tips

These tips are intended to help students and parents/guardians to successfully complete *The Next Chapter*® workbook.

01
TAKE YOUR TIME.
Don't try to complete The Next Chapter in one sitting. Give yourself enough time to identify, analyze, evaluate, and finalize school choices.

02
UNDERSTAND YOUR NEEDS.
Choosing a college should be based on your needs not brand. Your choices should be based on careers that you would like to pursue when completing a college degree.

03
KNOW YOUR WANTS.
It is okay to consider all the factors when choosing your fit. For example ask yourself: Do I like cold weather? Can I take my car? Would I like to attend a small or large school? How far from home would I consider?

04
THINK ABOUT YOUR FUTURE.
Make a timeline of your college and career goals.

05
TAKE NOTES THROUGHOUT THIS JOURNEY.
There will be a lot to remember. Take notes so you can compare your options at a later date. Taking notes will save you valuable time. You will feel more prepared and confident in making your decision.

06
RESEARCH ADMISSION STANDARDS.
Understand all of the admission requirements. Most schools have alternative admission requirements for students who do not meet admission standards.

07
FIND A SUPPORT SYSTEM.
You are not alone! There are other students in your area who are preparing to go to college. Locate students who previously attended your college choice (alumni). Don't be afraid to ask them questions.

08
TOUR THE CAMPUS.
Contact college recruitment offices to schedule tours in advance. Check to see if there are scheduled times for tours or if individualized tours can be arranged, and make an appointment.

09
KEEP TRACK OF IMPORTANT DATES.
It is important to meet all deadlines. Most schools have deadlines and do not grant extensions. Use a calendar to track important dates.

10
KEEP COPIES OF IMPORTANT DOCUMENTS.
Most schools require copies of students' personal documents. Keep a copy in your personal file in case documents are misplaced or you need them for other purposes.

About You

Having information readily available will make completing applications much easier. Complete the information below about yourself to capture an accurate snapshot of you! Most of the information will be used to complete admission and financial applications.

NAME		
STREET ADDRESS		
CITY	**STATE**	**ZIP**
COUNTY	**HOME PHONE**	
SOCIAL SECURITY NUMBER *(Do not write your SSN in this book! Memorize your social security number. Some college applications may require your Social Security Number)*	**CELL PHONE**	

STUDENT EMAIL *(Note: If your email name caters to your friends or it is a "fun" e-mail address, create a new email account. Use emails that are professional. Good Examples: ctaylor@xxxx.com , carltaylor@xxxx.com, c.taylor@xxxx.com; Avoid Examples: misscute@xxxx.com, hitmeup@xxxx.com, iloveme@xxxx.com*

SOCIAL MEDIA *(Tip: Most schools will have social media pages to communicate with students and parents, create a page for school purposes. Keep your page presentable and clean.)*

(f) _____   (twitter) _____

(instagram) _____   (snapchat) _____

(g+) _____   (youtube) _____

(in) _____   Other: _____

CURRENT HIGH SCHOOL		
SCHOOL ADDRESS		
CITY	STATE	ZIP
DISTRICT	SCHOOL PHONE NUMBER	

CURRENT COUNSELOR	
EMAIL ADDRESS	PHONE NUMBER
OFFICE HOURS	

CURRENT GRADE LEVEL	GPA	CLASS RANK	GRADUATION DATE

EXTRA-CURRICULAR ACTIVITIES

ACTIVITY 1	YEARS PARTICIPATED	POSITION
DUTIES	RECOGNITION/AWARDS	

ACTIVITY 2	YEARS PARTICIPATED	POSITION
DUTIES	RECOGNITION/AWARDS	

ACTIVITY 3	YEARS PARTICIPATED	POSITION
DUTIES	RECOGNITION/AWARDS	

ACTIVITY 4	YEARS PARTICIPATED	POSITION
DUTIES	RECOGNITION/AWARDS	

ACTIVITY 5	YEARS PARTICIPATED	POSITION
DUTIES	RECOGNITION/AWARDS	

ACTIVITY 6	YEARS PARTICIPATED	POSITION
DUTIES	RECOGNITION/AWARDS	

OTHER AWARDS/RECOGNITION

_____
_____
_____
_____

PARENTAL BACKGROUND

MOTHER'S COMPLETE NAME		
MOTHER'S ADDRESS		
CITY	STATE	ZIP
EMAIL	PHONE NUMBER	
HIGHEST EDUCATION LEVEL COMPLETED BY YOUR MOTHER		

FATHER'S COMPLETE NAME		
FATHER'S ADDRESS		|„
CITY	STATE	ZIP
EMAIL	PHONE NUMBER	
HIGHEST EDUCATION LEVEL COMPLETED BY YOUR FATHER		

College Entrance Exams

HAVE YOU TAKEN THE ACT? Yes ◯ No ◯ *If so, how many times?* _____

HAVE YOU TAKEN THE SAT? Yes ◯ No ◯ *If so, how many times?* _____
(See College Entrance Exam page to track scores)

HAVE YOU TAKEN ANY ADVANCED PLACEMENT (AP) COURSES? Yes ◯ No ◯	*If so, please list courses?* _____ _____ _____
HAVE YOU TAKEN ANY INTERNATIONAL BACCALAUREATE (IB) COURSES? Yes ◯ No ◯	*If so, please list courses?* _____ _____ _____
HAVE YOU TAKEN ANY DUAL-ENROLLMENT COURSES? Yes ◯ No ◯	*If so, please list courses?* _____ _____ _____
HAVE YOU TAKEN ANY DUAL-CREDIT COURSES? Yes ◯ No ◯	*If so, please list courses?* _____ _____ _____

Community Organizations

ORGANIZATION 1 _____ POSITION HELD _____
DUTIES _____

ORGANIZATION 2 _____ POSITION HELD _____
DUTIES _____

ORGANIZATION 3 _____ POSITION HELD _____
DUTIES _____

Jobs

JOB 1 _____ POSITION HELD _____
DUTIES _____
_____

JOB 2 _____ POSITION HELD _____
DUTIES _____
_____

JOB 3 _____ POSITION HELD _____
DUTIES _____
_____

INTERESTS *What do you want to learn?*

HOBBIES *What do you like to do in your spare time?*

Career Goals

What do you want to be when you grow up?
Think about things that you like to do or jobs that may interest you.
(Tip: Use the library or internet to research occupations and complete a career assessment.)

```
┌─────────────────────────────────────────────────────────┐
│                                                         │
│                                                         │
│                                                         │
└─────────────────────────────────────────────────────────┘
```

Top 5 Careers

01 _____ *What major relates to this career?* _____

02 _____ *What major relates to this career?* _____

03 _____ *What major relates to this career?* _____

04 _____ *What major relates to this career?* _____

05 _____ *What major relates to this career?* _____

Majors
What are the top 3 areas that interest you most?

01 _____

02 _____

03 _____

Minors
Second choice of study during undergraduate studies (Optional)

01 _____

02 _____

03 _____

Which School?

What's the best choice for you?

There are so many factors to consider when choosing your perfect fit.
Take time to think about location, distance, type, size, and cost.

- Where do you want to attend school?
- What type of school woud you like to attend?
    - *State College/University*
    - *Private College*
    - *Community/Junior College*
    - *Online College/University*
    - *Technical College*
    - *Vocational/Career College*

DO YOU PREFER TO STAY IN-STATE? Yes ◯ No ◯

DO YOU PREFER TO MOVE OUT-OF-STATE? Yes ◯ No ◯

IN WHICH STATES WOULD YOU CONSIDER ATTENDING SCHOOL?
(Tip: Use a web mapping service to find the distance from your state to that college. Ex: Google Maps.)

01 _____ *How far is this state from your home?* _____
02 _____ *How far is this state from your home?* _____
03 _____ *How far is this state from your home?* _____
04 _____ *How far is this state from your home?* _____
05 _____ *How far is this state from your home?* _____

(Tip: Most public or state colleges have out-of-state fees in addition to tuition. Make sure you ask if they offer out-of-state waivers.)

Types of Colleges
Choose the type(s) of colleges that may interest you. (Refer to the glossary for the description of types of colleges.)

◯ **STATE COLLEGE/UNIVERSITY**
◯ **PRIVATE COLLEGE**
◯ **COMMUNITY/JUNIOR COLLEGE**
◯ **ONLINE COLLEGE/UNIVERSITY**
◯ **TECHNICAL COLLEGE**
◯ **VOCATIONAL/CAREER COLLEGE**

Preferred Campus Size
(Tip: Consider your high-school, would you like a larger or smaller environment?)

◯ **SMALL** *(1000 students or less)*
◯ **MEDIUM** *(1000 – 10,000 students)*
◯ **LARGE** *(10,000 students or more)*
◯ **NO PREFERENCE**

Test Time!

College Entrance Exams

Most schools require students to take entrance exams for admission. Track the type, date, location, and scores of each college entrance exam as you complete them. Entrance exams may include:
- PSAT/NMSQT
- SAT Test
- SAT Subject Tests (Most Common)
- ACT (Most Common)

Tip: ACT Subscores (Critical Reading, Math, Science, Writing)
SAT Subscores (Critical Reading, Math, Writing)

Tip: Test schedules
- **PSAT**: *Sophomore of Junior years in high school (Usually scheduled by the high school)*
- **SAT**: *7 times per year (Oct, Nov, Dec, Jan, Mar or Apr, May and June)*
- **SAT Subject Area**: *(Oct, Nov, Dec, Jan, May and June)*
- **ACT**: *6 times per year (Sept, Oct, Dec, Feb, April, and June)*

Exams

TEST 1	DATE OF TEST	LOCATION

SCORE	SUBSCORES	
	Subject Area	*Score*

TEST 2	DATE OF TEST	LOCATION

SCORE	SUBSCORES	
	Subject Area	*Score*

TEST 3	DATE OF TEST	LOCATION

SCORE	SUBSCORES	
	Subject Area	*Score*

TEST DATES TO REMEMBER

TEST	DATE	COST

Do the Math!

Financial Sources

Financial sources may include scholarships, grants, loans, military assistance savings and gifts. Keep track of all possible financial sources. Complete the necessary paperwork on time. Be aware of the due dates, plan accordingly, and be mindful of terms and conditions.

- Have you completed the Free Application for Federal Student Aid (FAFSA)?
  DEADLINE TO COMPLETE:

- Give yourself a personal deadline prior to the required deadline.
  PERSONAL DEADLINE:

Steps to apply for the *Free Application for Federal Student Aid (FAFSA)*

- Locate someone that can assist in completing the application. This may include your high school counselor, financial aid counselor, community organizations or US Department of Education **1-800-4-FEDAID**.
- Gather required documents to complete the application.
  - Previous yearly tax returns (Beginning October 2016 students will be allowed to file the FAFSA using prior-prior year (PPY) tax information. The Class of 2017 will be the first high school graduates to fill the FAFSA using Prior-Prior Year (PPY)
  - W-2 Forms
  - Other income received
- Go to www.fafsa.ed.gov to complete the application.
  - Application is always FREE
  - Never pay anyone to assist you in completing the application
- Choose the appropriate application to complete
  - Options: State a New FAFSA or Returning User
    - First time users choose New FAFSA
    - To return to make corrections, add a school or view your student report choose Returning User
- Enter the requested information about you and your parents/guardians
- Enter your financial information
- You can choose up to 10 schools to send your Student Aid Report (SAR)
  - Take advantage of all schools
- Sign the application with your PIN.

Types of Funding Sources

01 SCHOLARSHIPS
Type of financial aid usually based on merit and needs.

02 GRANTS
Type of financial aid based on need. Student does not have to pay back.

03 LOANS
Type of financial aid that must be repaid with interest.
- Stafford
- Perkins
- Plus
- Private Student Loans

04 MILITARY FINANCIAL ASSISTANCE
Funds available for students from parent participation in the military.

05 SAVINGS
Money that is saved to pay for college expenses.

06 GIFTS
Money that is given to you to pay for college. *May be from a family member, friend, church, organization etc.*

Funding Sources

TYPE OF FUNDING 1			
DEADLINE TO APPLY	DATE APPLIED	DATE AWARDED	AMOUNT OF FUNIDNG
TERMS & CONDITIONS			

TYPE OF FUNDING 2			
DEADLINE TO APPLY	DATE APPLIED	DATE AWARDED	AMOUNT OF FUNIDNG
TERMS & CONDITIONS			

TYPE OF FUNDING 3			
DEADLINE TO APPLY	DATE APPLIED	DATE AWARDED	AMOUNT OF FUNIDNG
TERMS & CONDITIONS			

TYPE OF FUNDING 4			
DEADLINE TO APPLY	DATE APPLIED	DATE AWARDED	AMOUNT OF FUNIDNG
TERMS & CONDITIONS			

FINANCIAL AID CODES FOR FAFSA *(Use the Federal School Code Search to search for schools, look on the school's website or contact the financial aid office)*

SCHOOL	CODE

Scholarships

There are different types of scholarships for every student. Use the space below to track your scholarship opportunities. Scholarships may come from individuals, communities, schools, employers, non-profits, private companies, religious groups, and professional and social organizations. Write the information down for each scholarship, so it will be easy to follow up and complete in a timely manner. **Remember:** Watch your deadlines!

Scholarships to consider:

- *Need-Based Scholarships:* awarded based on the student and parent financial background
- *Merit-Based:* awarded based on academics and talents
- *School/Donor:* awarded from a school or private donor
- *Athletic:* awarded based on athletic ability
- *State Aid:* awarded by the state in which you reside
- *Community:* awarded based on leadership and community service
- *Church:* awarded based on commitment and involvement in your religious faith
- *Minority:* awarded to smaller groups that are enrolled

Scholarship Options

SCHOLARSHIP NAME 1		
TYPE OF SCHOLARSHIP		
DEADLINE	GPA REQUIREMENTS	STANDARDIZED TEST REQUIREMENT
LETTERS OF RECOMMENDATION		
OTHER REQUIREMENTS		
NOTES		
CONTACT PERSON'S NAME		CONTACT PERSON'S NUMBER

SCHOLARSHIP NAME 2		
TYPE OF SCHOLARSHIP		
DEADLINE	GPA REQUIREMENTS	STANDARDIZED TEST REQUIREMENT
LETTERS OF RECOMMENDATION		
OTHER REQUIREMENTS		
NOTES		
CONTACT PERSON'S NAME		CONTACT PERSON'S NUMBER

SCHOLARSHIP NAME 3		
TYPE OF SCHOLARSHIP		
DEADLINE	GPA REQUIREMENTS	STANDARDIZED TEST REQUIREMENT
LETTERS OF RECOMMENDATION		
OTHER REQUIREMENTS		
NOTES		
CONTACT PERSON'S NAME		CONTACT PERSON'S NUMBER

SCHOLARSHIP NAME 4		
TYPE OF SCHOLARSHIP		
DEADLINE	GPA REQUIREMENTS	STANDARDIZED TEST REQUIREMENT
LETTERS OF RECOMMENDATION		
OTHER REQUIREMENTS		
NOTES		
CONTACT PERSON'S NAME		CONTACT PERSON'S NUMBER

SCHOLARSHIP NAME 5		
TYPE OF SCHOLARSHIP		
DEADLINE	GPA REQUIREMENTS	STANDARDIZED TEST REQUIREMENT
LETTERS OF RECOMMENDATION		
OTHER REQUIREMENTS		
NOTES		
CONTACT PERSON'S NAME		CONTACT PERSON'S NUMBER

Application Process

How to Apply

Locate the application (Application forms can typically be found in the admission section on the school's website), or if you have a hard copy application, then, you are good to go.

- Determine if there is an application fee and whether or not you will need to pay via personal check, money order, or credit card.
- Read through the application before filling it out.
- Note any important information you need to gather prior to completing the application.
- Note essays or additional requirements of the application.
- Find a quiet spot to work on your application. Be diligent, focused, and neat. Double check your grammar and spelling.
- If an essay is required, take time to write a rough draft. Then, rewrite it before attaching it to your application. Be willing to go the extra mile to prove your abilities.
- If recommendations are required, print out necessary forms and decide who will give you the most glowing recommendation. Determine if they are to mail the recommendations in separately or attach them to your application. Will they need envelopes and stamps? If so, supply them. Be sure to allow them enough time to complete the form. After the recommendation letters have been sent, write and send those who completed a recommendation a thank-you note for their time and willingness to assist you.
- Make a copy of all paperwork before submitting the completed documents.
- Do your best!
- Submit either online or via hard copy with the United States Postal Service (USPS). Be mindful of due dates and allow enough time to get your paperwork in by deadlines.

Top 5 Colleges/ Universities

Identify & Breakdown

There are so many schools to choose from. Choose a college that matches five of the 10 descriptors. It is recommended that you identify at least five schools. *Your choices can include the following: two-year (community), four-year (public or private), online, vocational, technical, performing arts, etc.*

NOTE: Descriptors may be replaced to research schools that you are interested in.

The Starting 5

Carefully read the descriptor list below and choose five schools to begin your breakdown.

DESCRIPTORS	YOUR CHOICE
01	
02	
03	
04	
05	

Descriptors

DREAM SCHOOL School that you dreamed of going to as a child, saw it on TV, great athletic team, don't know anything about it, no connections, love the school colors	**HOMETOWN COMMUNITY COLLEGE** Community college located in or near your hometown
LEGACY FAMILY/ALUMNI SCHOOL School that family members or close friends of the family promote, attended, want everyone in the family to attend	**MOST POPULAR IN HIGH SCHOOL** Everyone at school is talking about attending, best friend may be attending
HOMETOWN SCHOOL School located in or near your hometown **STATE COLLEGE/UNIVERSITY** School located in your state	**IVY LEAGUE SCHOOL/FLAGSHIPS** Schools known for having high academic and social prestige located in the Eastern U.S. The eight Ivy League institutions are Brown University, Columbia University, Cornell University, Dartmouth College, Harvard University, the University of Pennsylvania, Princeton University, and Yale University.
PARTY SCHOOL School that is known for its fun factor	**SCHOOL LOCATED OUT-OF-STATE** School located outside of your state
SCHOOL OF YOUR CHOICE Choose a school that you may be interested in learning about	**BONUS** School of your choice

SCHOOL 1   DESCRIPTOR: _____

24

Research information using the internet and/or library, or find available information in the counseling office at your school. Fill out the form for each of the five colleges/universities you identified in the previous exercise. Most information can be located on the school's website.

SCHOOL'S NAME	

STUDENT POPULATION	DATE SCHEDULED FOR HIGH SCHOOL CAMPUS TOUR(S)

SCHOOL'S MISSION STATEMENT

TYPE OF SCHOOL *(Public/State, Private, Online, Vocational, Technical, Community/Junior)*	TOWN'S POPULATION *(Where the college is located?)*

SCHOOL'S ADDRESS

CITY	STATE	ZIP

DISTANCE FROM HOME *(Use a map search tool to determine the mileage.)*

TRAVEL TIME FROM YOUR HOME TO THE SCHOOL *(Use a map search tool to determine the travel time.)*

AUTOMOBILE	TRAIN	BUS	PLANE

TIME ZONE	SCHOOL'S WEBSITE

PHONE NUMBERS

MAIN CAMPUS	ADMISSION
FINANCIAL AID	**DEPARTMENT YOU ARE INTERESTED IN**

SCHOOL'S SOCIAL MEDIA

(f) _____   (t) _____

(in) _____   (▶) _____

(g+) _____   Other: _____

RELIGIOUS AFFILIATION *(If applicable)*

PREFERRED MAJOR _____

DOES THIS SCHOOL OFFER YOUR PREFERRED MAJOR?   Yes ◯   No ◯

IF NO, ARE YOU WILLING TO CHANGE YOUR MAJOR?   Yes ◯   No ◯

If no, eliminate this school. If yes, continue.

PREFERRED MINOR _____

Estimated Expenses

	FALL	SPRING	YEARLY TOTAL
TUITION			
In-state			
Out-of-state			
HOUSING			
Single			
Double			
OTHER FEES			
Meal Plan			
Mailbox Rental			
Books/Supplies			
Health Insurance			
Activity Fee			
Technology Fee			
Capital Improvement Fee			
TOTAL EXPENSES			

*Other fees may include: Travel Expenses (associated with traveling to and from campus to your family's place of residence at the start/end of the year and for holidays), etc.

Admission Requirements

SCHOOL REQUIREMENT	SCHOOL AVERAGE	YOURS
GPA		
SAT		
ACT		

AVAILABLE SCHOLARSHIPS

ARE THERE ANY SCHOLARSHIPS AVAILABLE? Yes ◯ No ◯

If so, what is the deadline? _____

ARE THERE ANY ESSAY(S) REQUIRED? Yes ◯ No ◯

If so, what is the deadline? _____

TOPIC 1	TOPIC 2	TOPIC 3

ARE THERE ALTERNATIVE ADMISSION REQUIREMENTS? Yes ◯ No ◯

If so, what are the requirements? _____
_____
_____

(Note: If you are an athlete, check NCAA requirements for incoming freshmen.)

What's next?

Now, it's time to request general information from the school. Fill out a form online on the college website or call the admission office. Determine how long it will take to get the requested information.

DATE REQUESTED _____ **DATE RECEIVED** _____

DOES THIS SCHOOL HAVE MY PREFERRED MAJOR? Yes ◯ No ◯	**DOES THIS SCHOOL HAVE MY PREFERRED MINOR?** Yes ◯ No ◯
IS THIS SCHOOL TOO FAR FROM HOME? Yes ◯ No ◯	**DO I MEET THE STANDARD ADMISSION REQUIREMENTS?** Yes ◯ No ◯
IS THERE AN ESSAY REQUIRED? Yes ◯ No ◯ *If so, what is the topic?* _____ _____	**DO I NEED RECOMMENDATION LETTERS?** Yes ◯ No ◯ *If so, how many and by whom?* _____ _____

DO MY PARENTS/GUARDIANS APPROVE OF THIS SCHOOL? Yes ◯ No ◯

APPLICATION DEADLINE	
APPLICATION FEE	
DATE APPLIED	
DATE ACCEPTED	
DATE DENIED	

ALTERNATIVE ADMISSION REQUIREMENTS

Notes

SCHOOL 2   DESCRIPTOR:_____ 28

Research information using the internet and/or library, or find available information in the counseling office at your school. Fill out the form for each of the five colleges/universities you identified in the previous exercise. Most information can be located on the school's website.

SCHOOL'S NAME	

STUDENT POPULATION	DATE SCHEDULED FOR HIGH SCHOOL CAMPUS TOUR(S)

SCHOOL'S MISSION STATEMENT

TYPE OF SCHOOL (Public/State, Private, Online, Vocational, Technical, Community/Junior)	TOWN'S POPULATION (Where the college is located?)

SCHOOL'S ADDRESS

CITY	STATE	ZIP

DISTANCE FROM HOME (Use a map search tool to determine the mileage.)

TRAVEL TIME FROM YOUR HOME TO THE SCHOOL (Use a map search tool to determine the travel time.)

AUTOMOBILE	TRAIN	BUS	PLANE

TIME ZONE	SCHOOL'S WEBSITE

PHONE NUMBERS

MAIN CAMPUS	ADMISSION
FINANCIAL AID	DEPARTMENT YOU ARE INTERESTED IN

SCHOOL'S SOCIAL MEDIA

(f) _____   (twitter) _____

(in) _____   (youtube) _____

(g+) _____   Other: _____

RELIGIOUS AFFILIATION *(If applicable)*
PREFERRED MAJOR _____ DOES THIS SCHOOL OFFER YOUR PREFERRED MAJOR? Yes ◯ No ◯ IF NO, ARE YOU WILLING TO CHANGE YOUR MAJOR? Yes ◯ No ◯ *If no, eliminate this school. If yes, continue.* PREFERRED MINOR _____

Estimated Expenses

	FALL	SPRING	YEARLY TOTAL
TUITION			
In-state			
Out-of-state			
HOUSING			
Single			
Double			
OTHER FEES			
Meal Plan			
Mailbox Rental			
Books/Supplies			
Health Insurance			
Activity Fee			
Technology Fee			
Capital Improvement Fee			
TOTAL EXPENSES			

*Other fees may include: Travel Expenses (associated with traveling to and from campus to your family's place of residence at the start/end of the year and for holidays), etc.

Admission Requirements

SCHOOL REQUIREMENT	SCHOOL AVERAGE	YOURS
GPA		
SAT		
ACT		

AVAILABLE SCHOLARSHIPS

ARE THERE ANY SCHOLARSHIPS AVAILABLE? Yes ◯ No ◯

If so, what is the deadline? _____

ARE THERE ANY ESSAY(S) REQUIRED? Yes ◯ No ◯

If so, what is the deadline? _____

TOPIC 1	TOPIC 2	TOPIC 3

ARE THERE ALTERNATIVE ADMISSION REQUIREMENTS? Yes ◯ No ◯

If so, what are the requirements? _____
_____
_____

(Note: If you are an athlete, check NCAA requirements for incoming freshmen.)

What's next?

Now, it's time to request general information from the school. Fill out a form on-line on the college website or call the admission office. Determine how long it will take to get the requested information.

DATE REQUESTED _____ **DATE RECEIVED** _____

DOES THIS SCHOOL HAVE MY PREFERRED MAJOR? Yes ◯ No ◯	**DOES THIS SCHOOL HAVE MY PREFERRED MINOR?** Yes ◯ No ◯
IS THIS SCHOOL TOO FAR FROM HOME? Yes ◯ No ◯	**DO I MEET THE STANDARD ADMISSION REQUIREMENTS?** Yes ◯ No ◯
IS THERE AN ESSAY REQUIRED? Yes ◯ No ◯ *If so, what is the topic?* _____ _____	**DO I NEED RECOMMENDATION LETTERS?** Yes ◯ No ◯ *If so, how many and by whom?* _____ _____

DO MY PARENTS/GUARDIANS APPROVE OF THIS SCHOOL? Yes ◯ No ◯

APPLICATION DEADLINE	_____
APPLICATION FEE	_____
DATE APPLIED	_____
DATE ACCEPTED	_____
DATE DENIED	_____

ALTERNATIVE ADMISSION REQUIREMENTS

Notes

SCHOOL 3 DESCRIPTOR: _____

Research information using the internet and/or library, or find available information in the counseling office at your school. Fill out the form for each of the five colleges/universities you identified in the previous exercise. Most information can be located on the school's website.

SCHOOL'S NAME	
STUDENT POPULATION	**DATE SCHEDULED FOR HIGH SCHOOL CAMPUS TOUR(S)**
SCHOOL'S MISSION STATEMENT	
TYPE OF SCHOOL *(Public/State, Private, Online, Vocational, Technical, Community/Junior)*	**TOWN'S POPULATION** *(Where the college is located?)*

SCHOOL'S ADDRESS

CITY	STATE	ZIP

DISTANCE FROM HOME *(Use a map search tool to determine the mileage.)*

TRAVEL TIME FROM YOUR HOME TO THE SCHOOL *(Use a map search tool to determine the travel time.)*

AUTOMOBILE	TRAIN	BUS	PLANE

TIME ZONE	SCHOOL'S WEBSITE

PHONE NUMBERS

MAIN CAMPUS	ADMISSION
FINANCIAL AID	**DEPARTMENT YOU ARE INTERESTED IN**

SCHOOL'S SOCIAL MEDIA

(f) _____   (twitter) _____

(in) _____   (youtube) _____

(g+) _____   Other: _____

RELIGIOUS AFFILIATION *(If applicable)*

PREFERRED MAJOR _____

DOES THIS SCHOOL OFFER YOUR PREFERRED MAJOR?   Yes ◯   No ◯

IF NO, ARE YOU WILLING TO CHANGE YOUR MAJOR?   Yes ◯   No ◯

If no, eliminate this school. If yes, continue.

PREFERRED MINOR _____

Estimated Expenses

	FALL	SPRING	YEARLY TOTAL
TUITION			
In-state			
Out-of-state			
HOUSING			
Single			
Double			
OTHER FEES			
Meal Plan			
Mailbox Rental			
Books/Supplies			
Health Insurance			
Activity Fee			
Technology Fee			
Capital Improvement Fee			
TOTAL EXPENSES			

*Other fees may include: Travel Expenses (associated with traveling to and from campus to your family's place of residence at the start/end of the year and for holidays), etc.

Admission Requirements

SCHOOL REQUIREMENT	SCHOOL AVERAGE	YOURS
GPA		
SAT		
ACT		

AVAILABLE SCHOLARSHIPS

ARE THERE ANY SCHOLARSHIPS AVAILABLE? Yes ◯ No ◯

If so, what is the deadline? _____

ARE THERE ANY ESSAY(S) REQUIRED? Yes ◯ No ◯

If so, what is the deadline? _____

TOPIC 1	TOPIC 2	TOPIC 3

ARE THERE ALTERNATIVE ADMISSION REQUIREMENTS? Yes ◯ No ◯

If so, what are the requirements? _____
_____
_____

(Note: If you are an athlete, check NCAA requirements for incoming freshmen.)

What's next?

Now, it's time to request general information from the school. Fill out a form on-line on the college website or call the admission office. Determine how long it will take to get the requested information.

DATE REQUESTED _____ **DATE RECEIVED** _____

DOES THIS SCHOOL HAVE MY PREFERRED MAJOR? Yes ◯ No ◯	**DOES THIS SCHOOL HAVE MY PREFERRED MINOR?** Yes ◯ No ◯
IS THIS SCHOOL TOO FAR FROM HOME? Yes ◯ No ◯	**DO I MEET THE STANDARD ADMISSION REQUIREMENTS?** Yes ◯ No ◯
IS THERE AN ESSAY REQUIRED? Yes ◯ No ◯ *If so, what is the topic?* _____ _____	**DO I NEED RECOMMENDATION LETTERS?** Yes ◯ No ◯ *If so, how many and by whom?* _____ _____

DO MY PARENTS/GUARDIANS APPROVE OF THIS SCHOOL? Yes ◯ No ◯

APPLICATION DEADLINE	_____
APPLICATION FEE	_____
DATE APPLIED	_____
DATE ACCEPTED	_____
DATE DENIED	_____

ALTERNATIVE ADMISSION REQUIREMENTS

_____

_____

Notes

SCHOOL 4 DESCRIPTOR: _____ 36

Research information using the internet and/or library, or find available information in the counseling office at your school. Fill out the form for each of the five colleges/universities you identified in the previous exercise. Most information can be located on the school's website.

SCHOOL'S NAME

STUDENT POPULATION	**DATE SCHEDULED FOR HIGH SCHOOL CAMPUS TOUR(S)**

SCHOOL'S MISSION STATEMENT

TYPE OF SCHOOL (Public/State, Private, Online, Vocational, Technical, Community/Junior)	**TOWN'S POPULATION** (Where the college is located?)

SCHOOL'S ADDRESS

CITY	**STATE**	**ZIP**

DISTANCE FROM HOME (Use a map search tool to determine the mileage.)

TRAVEL TIME FROM YOUR HOME TO THE SCHOOL (Use a map search tool to determine the travel time.)

AUTOMOBILE	**TRAIN**	**BUS**	**PLANE**

TIME ZONE	**SCHOOL'S WEBSITE**

PHONE NUMBERS

MAIN CAMPUS	**ADMISSION**
FINANCIAL AID	**DEPARTMENT YOU ARE INTERESTED IN**

SCHOOL'S SOCIAL MEDIA

(f) _____ (t) _____

(in) _____ (yt) _____

(g+) _____ Other: _____

RELIGIOUS AFFILIATION *(If applicable)*

PREFERRED MAJOR _____

DOES THIS SCHOOL OFFER YOUR PREFERRED MAJOR?   Yes ◯ No ◯

IF NO, ARE YOU WILLING TO CHANGE YOUR MAJOR?   Yes ◯ No ◯

If no, eliminate this school. If yes, continue.

PREFERRED MINOR _____

Estimated Expenses

	FALL	SPRING	YEARLY TOTAL
TUITION			
In-state			
Out-of-state			
HOUSING			
Single			
Double			
OTHER FEES			
Meal Plan			
Mailbox Rental			
Books/Supplies			
Health Insurance			
Activity Fee			
Technology Fee			
Capital Improvement Fee			
TOTAL EXPENSES			

*Other fees may include: Travel Expenses (associated with traveling to and from campus to your family's place of residence at the start/end of the year and for holidays), etc.

Admission Requirements

SCHOOL REQUIREMENT	SCHOOL AVERAGE	YOURS
GPA		
SAT		
ACT		

AVAILABLE SCHOLARSHIPS

ARE THERE ANY SCHOLARSHIPS AVAILABLE? Yes ◯ No ◯

If so, what is the deadline? _____

ARE THERE ANY ESSAY(S) REQUIRED? Yes ◯ No ◯

If so, what is the deadline? _____

TOPIC 1	TOPIC 2	TOPIC 3

ARE THERE ALTERNATIVE ADMISSION REQUIREMENTS? Yes ◯ No ◯

If so, what are the requirements? _____
_____
_____

(Note: If you are an athlete, check NCAA requirements for incoming freshmen.)

What's next?

Now, it's time to request general information from the school. Fill out a form on-line on the college website or call the admission office. Determine how long it will take to get the requested information.

DATE REQUESTED _____   **DATE RECEIVED** _____

DOES THIS SCHOOL HAVE MY PREFERRED MAJOR? Yes ◯ No ◯	**DOES THIS SCHOOL HAVE MY PREFERRED MINOR?** Yes ◯ No ◯
IS THIS SCHOOL TOO FAR FROM HOME? Yes ◯ No ◯	**DO I MEET THE STANDARD ADMISSION REQUIREMENTS?** Yes ◯ No ◯
IS THERE AN ESSAY REQUIRED? Yes ◯ No ◯ *If so, what is the topic?* _____ _____	**DO I NEED RECOMMENDATION LETTERS?** Yes ◯ No ◯ *If so, how many and by whom?* _____ _____

DO MY PARENTS/GUARDIANS APPROVE OF THIS SCHOOL? Yes ◯ No ◯

APPLICATION DEADLINE	_____
APPLICATION FEE	_____
DATE APPLIED	_____
DATE ACCEPTED	_____
DATE DENIED	_____

ALTERNATIVE ADMISSION REQUIREMENTS

_____
_____

Notes

_____
_____
_____
_____
_____
_____
_____
_____
_____
_____
_____
_____
_____
_____
_____

SCHOOL 5 DESCRIPTOR: _____

40

Research information using the internet and/or library, or find available information in the counseling office at your school. Fill out the form for each of the five colleges/universities you identified in the previous exercise. Most information can be located on the school's website.

SCHOOL'S NAME	
STUDENT POPULATION	DATE SCHEDULED FOR HIGH SCHOOL CAMPUS TOUR(S)
SCHOOL'S MISSION STATEMENT	
TYPE OF SCHOOL (Public/State, Private, Online, Vocational, Technical, Community/Junior)	TOWN'S POPULATION (Where the college is located?)

SCHOOL'S ADDRESS

CITY	STATE	ZIP

DISTANCE FROM HOME (Use a map search tool to determine the mileage.)

TRAVEL TIME FROM YOUR HOME TO THE SCHOOL (Use a map search tool to determine the travel time.)

AUTOMOBILE	TRAIN	BUS	PLANE

TIME ZONE	SCHOOL'S WEBSITE

PHONE NUMBERS

MAIN CAMPUS	ADMISSION
FINANCIAL AID	DEPARTMENT YOU ARE INTERESTED IN

SCHOOL'S SOCIAL MEDIA

(f) _____   (twitter) _____

(in) _____   (youtube) _____

(g+) _____   Other: _____

RELIGIOUS AFFILIATION *(If applicable)*

PREFERRED MAJOR _____

DOES THIS SCHOOL OFFER YOUR PREFERRED MAJOR? Yes ◯ No ◯

IF NO, ARE YOU WILLING TO CHANGE YOUR MAJOR? Yes ◯ No ◯

If no, eliminate this school. If yes, continue.

PREFERRED MINOR _____

Estimated Expenses

	FALL	SPRING	YEARLY TOTAL
TUITION			
In-state			
Out-of-state			
HOUSING			
Single			
Double			
OTHER FEES			
Meal Plan			
Mailbox Rental			
Books/Supplies			
Health Insurance			
Activity Fee			
Technology Fee			
Capital Improvement Fee			
TOTAL EXPENSES			

*Other fees may include: Travel Expenses (associated with traveling to and from campus to your family's place of residence at the start/end of the year and for holidays), etc.

Admission Requirements

SCHOOL REQUIREMENT	SCHOOL AVERAGE	YOURS
GPA		
SAT		
ACT		

AVAILABLE SCHOLARSHIPS

ARE THERE ANY SCHOLARSHIPS AVAILABLE? Yes ◯ No ◯

If so, what is the deadline? _____

ARE THERE ANY ESSAY(S) REQUIRED? Yes ◯ No ◯

If so, what is the deadline? _____

TOPIC 1	TOPIC 2	TOPIC 3

ARE THERE ALTERNATIVE ADMISSION REQUIREMENTS? Yes ◯ No ◯

If so, what are the requirements? _____
_____
_____

(Note: If you are an athlete, check NCAA requirements for incoming freshmen.)

What's next?

Now, it's time to request general information from the school. Fill out a form on-line on the college website or call the admission office. Determine how long it will take to get the requested information.

DATE REQUESTED _____ **DATE RECEIVED** _____

DOES THIS SCHOOL HAVE MY PREFERRED MAJOR? Yes ◯ No ◯	**DOES THIS SCHOOL HAVE MY PREFERRED MINOR?** Yes ◯ No ◯
IS THIS SCHOOL TOO FAR FROM HOME? Yes ◯ No ◯	**DO I MEET THE STANDARD ADMISSION REQUIREMENTS?** Yes ◯ No ◯
IS THERE AN ESSAY REQUIRED? Yes ◯ No ◯ *If so, what is the topic?* _____ _____	**DO I NEED RECOMMENDATION LETTERS?** Yes ◯ No ◯ *If so, how many and by whom?* _____ _____

DO MY PARENTS/GUARDIANS APPROVE OF THIS SCHOOL? Yes ◯ No ◯

APPLICATION DEADLINE	
APPLICATION FEE	
DATE APPLIED	
DATE ACCEPTED	
DATE DENIED	

ALTERNATIVE ADMISSION REQUIREMENTS

Notes

Top 5 Choices

Comparison Chart

SCHOOL	LOCATION	SIZE	COST	DO YOU HAVE FINANCIALS SECURED?	HOW MUCH IS SECURED TOWARDS THE TOTAL COST?	DO YOU MEET ADMISSION REQUIREMENTS?
01				Yes ◯ No ◯		Yes ◯ No ◯
02				Yes ◯ No ◯		Yes ◯ No ◯
03				Yes ◯ No ◯		Yes ◯ No ◯
04				Yes ◯ No ◯		Yes ◯ No ◯
05				Yes ◯ No ◯		Yes ◯ No ◯

Now that you have an overview of your top five schools, you are ready to eliminate five. Take a look at each school and your overview answers. *Things to consider: Financials, Admission Requirements, Location, and Interests. Analyze, sit with an adult and eliminate.* **Remember: *You can only attend one school!***

Elimination Time!

SCHOOL	LOCATION
01	Keep ◯ Eliminate ◯
02	Keep ◯ Eliminate ◯
03	Keep ◯ Eliminate ◯
04	Keep ◯ Eliminate ◯
05	Keep ◯ Eliminate ◯

Top 3 Choices

SCHOOL
01
02
03

Top 3 Colleges/ Universities

Let's break things down even more!

Now, it is time to narrow your choices down to the top three schools you would like to visit as your prospective college/university. Fill out a form for each of your Top 3. Research needed information using the internet, library, or materials from the college website, etc. Some of this information you have already listed in the previous activities.

SCHOOL 1

Research information using the internet and/or library, or find available information in the counseling office at your school. Fill out the form for each of the 5 colleges/universities you identified in the previous exercise. Most information can be located on the school's website.

SCHOOL'S NAME	STATE LOCATED
MAJOR	MINOR
TUITION COST	TRAVEL COST
TOTAL ESTIMATED COST PER YEAR	HOUSING APPLICATION FEE

TOTAL YEARLY COST _____ X ____ YEARS TO COMPLETE = _____ TOTAL COST TO COMPLETE DEGREE

DUE DATE FOR PAYMENT *Failure to make payments may affect future enrollments*	PAYMENT PLAN OPTIONS? Yes ◯ No ◯

Funding Sources

Have you completed the Free Application for Federal Student Aid (FAFSA)? Yes ◯ No ◯

COLLEGE/UNIVERSITY SCHOLARSHIPS

SCHOLARSHIP NAME 1	DEADLINE
LETTERS OF RECOMMENDATION	
GPA REQUIREMENTS	OTHER REQUIREMENTS

SCHOLARSHIP NAME 2	DEADLINE
LETTERS OF RECOMMENDATION	
GPA REQUIREMENTS	OTHER REQUIREMENTS

SCHOLARSHIP NAME 3	DEADLINE
LETTERS OF RECOMMENDATION	
GPA REQUIREMENTS	OTHER REQUIREMENTS

DEPARTMENT SCHOLARSHIPS

SCHOLARSHIP NAME 4	DEADLINE
LETTERS OF RECOMMENDATION	
GPA REQUIREMENTS	**OTHER REQUIREMENTS**

SCHOLARSHIP NAME 5	DEADLINE
LETTERS OF RECOMMENDATION	
GPA REQUIREMENTS	**OTHER REQUIREMENTS**

OTHER TYPES OF FUNDING

Do you have the financial means secured to attend this school? Yes ◯ No ◯

TYPE OF FUNDING 1		
DATE AWARDED	**AMOUNT OF FUNDING**	**DEADLINE TO SECURE FUNDING**
TERMS & CONDITIONS		

TYPE OF FUNDING 2		
DATE AWARDED	**AMOUNT OF FUNDING**	**DEADLINE TO SECURE FUNDING**
TERMS & CONDITIONS		

TYPE OF FUNDING 3		
DATE AWARDED	**AMOUNT OF FUNDING**	**DEADLINE TO SECURE FUNDING**
TERMS & CONDITIONS		

Academics

MAJOR	DEGREE I WILL RECEIVE
How many credit hours will I need to complete a degree?	How many years will it take to complete this degree?
MINOR	DEGREE I WILL RECEIVE
How many credit hours will I need to complete a degree?	How many years will it take to complete this degree?

Admission Requirements

Do you meet the standard admission requirements?   Yes ◯   No ◯
If not, are there alternative admission requirements? List alternative admission requirements.   _____   _____   _____
Is early admission available as an option?   Yes ◯   No ◯

(Note: You will need your academic transcript to complete the activity below. Request your transcript from your counselor or records clerk.)

CURRENT GPA	REQUIRED GPA FOR GIVEN COLLEGE

INCOMING FRESHMAN ADMISSION REQUIREMENTS

COURSES	REQUIRED CREDIT HOURS	COMPLETED
English		
Math		
Science		
History		
Foreign Language		
Advanced Elective(s)		
Arts		
Technology		
Other		
Other		

Most colleges have course requirements for incoming freshmen. Based on the requirements, look at your transcript and evaluate courses that you have completed. Place a final grade in the box, if you have completed it. Additional spaces are available.

NEED: CURRENT TRANSCRIPT

CURRENT GPA	REQUIRED GPA FOR GIVEN COLLEGE

		Check if completed.			
COURSES	9TH	10TH	11TH	12TH	How many does this college require?
English					
Math					
Science					
History					
Foreign Language					
Advanced Elective(s)					
Fine Arts					
Technology					
Economics					
Physical Education					
Health					
Speech					
Other					
Other					

*Add other course requirements and schedule an appointment with your counselor to discuss any courses or discrepancies that you need to complete high school graduation requirements.

PHONE LOGS FROM SCHOOL

DATE	PHONE NUMBER	PERSON YOU SPOKE TO	COMMENTS

Important Deadlines

Include deadlines for admissions, scholarships, financial aid, campus tours, college entrance exams, auditions, high school class days and other important dates.

EVENT	DATE OF EVENT	DEADLINE TO APPLY

APPLICATION DEADLINE	
APPLICATION FEE	
DATE APPLIED	
DATE ACCEPTED	
DATE DENIED	

ALTERNATIVE ADMISSION REQUIREMENTS

_____

_____

Notes

_____

_____

_____

_____

_____

_____

_____

SCHOOL 2

Research information using the internet and/or library, or find available information in the counseling office at your school. Fill out the form for each of the 5 colleges/universities you identified in the previous exercise. Most information can be located on the school's website.

SCHOOL'S NAME	STATE LOCATED
MAJOR	MINOR
TUITION COST	TRAVEL COST
TOTAL ESTIMATED COST PER YEAR	HOUSING APPLICATION FEE

TOTAL YEARLY COST _____ X ___ YEARS TO COMPLETE = _____ TOTAL COST TO COMPLETE DEGREE

DUE DATE FOR PAYMENT Failure to make payments may affect future enrollments	PAYMENT PLAN OPTIONS? Yes ◯ No ◯

Funding Sources

Have you completed the Free Application for Federal Student Aid (FAFSA)? Yes ◯ No ◯

COLLEGE/UNIVERSITY SCHOLARSHIPS

SCHOLARSHIP NAME 1	DEADLINE
LETTERS OF RECOMMENDATION	
GPA REQUIREMENTS	OTHER REQUIREMENTS

SCHOLARSHIP NAME 2	DEADLINE
LETTERS OF RECOMMENDATION	
GPA REQUIREMENTS	OTHER REQUIREMENTS

SCHOLARSHIP NAME 3	DEADLINE
LETTERS OF RECOMMENDATION	
GPA REQUIREMENTS	OTHER REQUIREMENTS

DEPARTMENT SCHOLARSHIPS

SCHOLARSHIP NAME 4	DEADLINE
LETTERS OF RECOMMENDATION	
GPA REQUIREMENTS	OTHER REQUIREMENTS

SCHOLARSHIP NAME 5	DEADLINE
LETTERS OF RECOMMENDATION	
GPA REQUIREMENTS	OTHER REQUIREMENTS

OTHER TYPES OF FUNDING

Do you have the financial means secured to attend this school? Yes ◯ No ◯

TYPE OF FUNDING 1		
DATE AWARDED	AMOUNT OF FUNDING	DEADLINE TO SECURE FUNDING
TERMS & CONDITIONS		

TYPE OF FUNDING 2		
DATE AWARDED	AMOUNT OF FUNDING	DEADLINE TO SECURE FUNDING
TERMS & CONDITIONS		

TYPE OF FUNDING 3		
DATE AWARDED	AMOUNT OF FUNDING	DEADLINE TO SECURE FUNDING
TERMS & CONDITIONS		

Academics

MAJOR	DEGREE I WILL RECEIVE
How many credit hours will I need to complete a degree?	How many years will it take to complete this degree?
MINOR	DEGREE I WILL RECEIVE
How many credit hours will I need to complete a degree?	How many years will it take to complete this degree?

Admission Requirements

Do you meet the standard admission requirements?   Yes ◯   No ◯
If not, are there alternative admission requirements? List alternative admission requirements.   _____   _____   _____
Is early admission available as an option?   Yes ◯   No ◯

(Note: You will need your academic transcript to complete the activity below. Request your transcript from your counselor or records clerk.)

CURRENT GPA	REQUIRED GPA FOR GIVEN COLLEGE

INCOMING FRESHMAN ADMISSION REQUIREMENTS

COURSES	REQUIRED CREDIT HOURS	COMPLETED
English		
Math		
Science		
History		
Foreign Language		
Advanced Elective(s)		
Arts		
Technology		
Other		
Other		

Most colleges have course requirements for incoming freshmen. Based on the requirements, look at your transcript and evaluate courses that you have completed. Place a final grade in the box, if you have completed it. Additional spaces are available.

NEED: CURRENT TRANSCRIPT

CURRENT GPA	REQUIRED GPA FOR GIVEN COLLEGE

COURSES	Check if completed.				How many does this college require?
	9TH	10TH	11TH	12TH	
English					
Math					
Science					
History					
Foreign Language					
Advanced Elective(s)					
Fine Arts					
Technology					
Economics					
Physical Education					
Health					
Speech					
Other					
Other					

*Add other course requirements and schedule an appointment with your counselor to discuss any courses or discrepancies that you need to complete high school graduation requirements.

PHONE LOGS FROM SCHOOL

DATE	PHONE NUMBER	PERSON YOU SPOKE TO	COMMENTS

Important Deadlines

Include deadlines for admissions, scholarships, financial aid, campus tours, college entrance exams, auditions, high school class days and other important dates.

EVENT	DATE OF EVENT	DEADLINE TO APPLY

APPLICATION DEADLINE	
APPLICATION FEE	
DATE APPLIED	
DATE ACCEPTED	
DATE DENIED	

ALTERNATIVE ADMISSION REQUIREMENTS

_____

_____

Notes

_____

_____

_____

_____

_____

_____

SCHOOL 3

Research information using the internet and/or library, or find available information in the counseling office at your school. Fill out the form for each of the 5 colleges/universities you identified in the previous exercise. Most information can be located on the school's website.

SCHOOL'S NAME	STATE LOCATED
MAJOR	**MINOR**
TUITION COST	**TRAVEL COST**
TOTAL ESTIMATED COST PER YEAR	**HOUSING APPLICATION FEE**

TOTAL YEARLY COST _____ X ____ **YEARS TO COMPLETE** = _____ **TOTAL COST TO COMPLETE DEGREE**

DUE DATE FOR PAYMENT *Failure to make payments may affect future enrollments*	**PAYMENT PLAN OPTIONS?** Yes ◯ No ◯

Funding Sources

Have you completed the Free Application for Federal Student Aid (FAFSA)? Yes ◯ No ◯

COLLEGE/UNIVERSITY SCHOLARSHIPS

SCHOLARSHIP NAME 1	**DEADLINE**
LETTERS OF RECOMMENDATION	
GPA REQUIREMENTS	**OTHER REQUIREMENTS**

SCHOLARSHIP NAME 2	**DEADLINE**
LETTERS OF RECOMMENDATION	
GPA REQUIREMENTS	**OTHER REQUIREMENTS**

SCHOLARSHIP NAME 3	**DEADLINE**
LETTERS OF RECOMMENDATION	
GPA REQUIREMENTS	**OTHER REQUIREMENTS**

DEPARTMENT SCHOLARSHIPS

SCHOLARSHIP NAME 4		DEADLINE
LETTERS OF RECOMMENDATION		
GPA REQUIREMENTS	OTHER REQUIREMENTS	

SCHOLARSHIP NAME 5		DEADLINE
LETTERS OF RECOMMENDATION		
GPA REQUIREMENTS	OTHER REQUIREMENTS	

OTHER TYPES OF FUNDING

Do you have the financial means secured to attend this school? Yes ◯ No ◯

TYPE OF FUNDING 1		
DATE AWARDED	AMOUNT OF FUNDING	DEADLINE TO SECURE FUNDING
TERMS & CONDITIONS		

TYPE OF FUNDING 2		
DATE AWARDED	AMOUNT OF FUNDING	DEADLINE TO SECURE FUNDING
TERMS & CONDITIONS		

TYPE OF FUNDING 3		
DATE AWARDED	AMOUNT OF FUNDING	DEADLINE TO SECURE FUNDING
TERMS & CONDITIONS		

Academics

MAJOR	DEGREE I WILL RECEIVE
How many credit hours will I need to complete a degree?	How many years will it take to complete this degree?
MINOR	DEGREE I WILL RECEIVE
How many credit hours will I need to complete a degree?	How many years will it take to complete this degree?

Admission Requirements

Do you meet the standard admission requirements? Yes ◯ No ◯

If not, are there alternative admission requirements? List alternative admission requirements.
_____
_____
_____

Is early admission available as an option? Yes ◯ No ◯

(Note: You will need your academic transcript to complete the activity below. Request your transcript from your counselor or records clerk.)

CURRENT GPA	REQUIRED GPA FOR GIVEN COLLEGE

INCOMING FRESHMAN ADMISSION REQUIREMENTS

COURSES	REQUIRED CREDIT HOURS	COMPLETED
English		
Math		
Science		
History		
Foreign Language		
Advanced Elective(s)		
Arts		
Technology		
Other		
Other		

Most colleges have course requirements for incoming freshmen. Based on the requirements, look at your transcript and evaluate courses that you have completed. Place a final grade in the box, if you have completed it. Additional spaces are available.

NEED: CURRENT TRANSCRIPT

CURRENT GPA	REQUIRED GPA FOR GIVEN COLLEGE

	Check if completed.				
COURSES	9TH	10TH	11TH	12TH	How many does this college require?
English					
Math					
Science					
History					
Foreign Language					
Advanced Elective(s)					
Fine Arts					
Technology					
Economics					
Physical Education					
Health					
Speech					
Other					
Other					

*Add other course requirements and schedule an appointment with your counselor to discuss any courses or discrepancies that you need to complete high school graduation requirements.

PHONE LOGS FROM SCHOOL

DATE	PHONE NUMBER	PERSON YOU SPOKE TO	COMMENTS

Important Deadlines

Include deadlines for admissions, scholarships, financial aid, campus tours, college entrance exams, auditions, high school class days and other important dates.

EVENT	DATE OF EVENT	DEADLINE TO APPLY

APPLICATION DEADLINE	
APPLICATION FEE	
DATE APPLIED	
DATE ACCEPTED	
DATE DENIED	

ALTERNATIVE ADMISSION REQUIREMENTS

_____

_____

Notes

_____

_____

_____

_____

_____

_____

Top 3 Choices

Comparison Chart

SCHOOL	LOCATION	SIZE	COST	DO YOU HAVE FINANCIALS SECURED?	HOW MUCH IS SECURED TOWARDS THE TOTAL COST?	DO YOU MEET ADMISSION REQUIREMENTS?
01				Yes ○ No ○		Yes ○ No ○
02				Yes ○ No ○		Yes ○ No ○
03				Yes ○ No ○		Yes ○ No ○

Now that you have an overview of your top 3 schools, you are ready to eliminate two. Take a look at each school and your overview answers. Things to consider: Financials, Admission Requirements, Location, and Interests. Analyze, sit with an adult and eliminate. **Remember: You can only attend one school!**

Elimination Time!

SCHOOL	LOCATION
01	Keep ○ Eliminate ○
02	Keep ○ Eliminate ○
03	Keep ○ Eliminate ○

Top Choice!

Congratulations!

You are ready to explore The Next Chapter of your life.

_____

I'm
Ready for
The Next Chapter®

College Choice

SCHOOL'S CONTACTS	
REGISTRAR CONTACTS	**TELEPHONE NUMBER**
DEPARTMENT CONTACTS	**TELEPHONE NUMBER**

ADVISOR'S NAME	ADVISOR'S TELEPHONE NUMBER
DATE APPLICATION COMPLETED AND MAILED IN	DATE ADMITTED/ACCEPTED/REJECTED
HAVE YOU COMPLETED THE FAFSA? Yes ◯ No ◯	FINANCIAL AID NUMBER

HAVE YOU APPLIED FOR HOUSING? Yes ◯ No ◯

If yes, dormitory preferred_____ dormitory assigned _____

FRESHMAN ORIENTATION DATE	NOTES
HAVE YOU MADE YOUR SCHEDULE? Yes ◯ No ◯	HOW MANY CREDIT HOURS ARE YOU TAKING?

CLASSES YOU HAVE REGISTERED FOR

1ST SEMESTER	PROFESSOR

MASCOT	

ENROLLMENT

APPLICATION DEADLINE	
APPLICATION COMPLETED	
ACCEPTED	

COST

TOTAL SCHOLARSHIPS OFFERED	
TOTAL FINANCIAL SAVINGS	
TOTAL GRANTS	
TOTAL STUDENT LOANS	
TOTAL ADDITIONAL LOANS	

ACADEMICS

ACADEMIC COUNSELOR	
FRESHMAN ORIENTATION DATE	

HOUSING

APPLICATION DEADLINE	
DORMITORY	
ROOMMATE	
ROOMMATE'S CONTACT INFORMATION	*Address:* *Phone #:* *Email:* *Social Media:*
MOVE-IN DATE	

Get to know the area where your school is located.
Make note of people and places that may be useful to you.

SAFETY & MEDICAL

POLICE STATION *(closest)*	
Name	
Address	
Phone Number	
FIRE STATION *(closest)*	
Name	
Address	
Phone Number	
HOSPITAL *(closest)*	
Name	
Address	
Phone Number	

SHOPPING

GROCERY STORE	**SUPERSTORES**

MALLS	CLOTHING STORES

HEALTH & BEAUTY

AFTER HOURS CLINIC (closest)	
Name	
Address	
Phone Number	
DENTAL OFFICE	
Name	
Address	
Phone Number	
BEAUTY SUPPLY/SALON/BARBER	
Name	
Address	
Phone Number	

RESTAURANTS/FAST FOOD

ENTERTAINMENT *(Movie Theatre, Fun Places, etc.)*

BOOK STORES

Academic Advisor/Counselor – an employee at an institution who assists in selecting the required courses necessary for graduation. This employee may also serve as a contact to address any academic issues.

academic calendar – calendar designed to show the day-to-day activities at an institution. Activities may include but not limited to: deadlines, admission dates, start/end dates, commencements , financial deadlines, orientations, holidays, and grading

academic probation – a warning to the student that their cumulative grade point average has fallen below the required average and they are not in "academic good standing" with the institution. Students are usually given an academic semester to show improvement

academic suspension - a period that a student is dismissed from an institution because their cumulative grade point average (GPA) has fallen below the required average. Students are usually given a warning prior to suspension.

academic year – the section of the year that an institution provides academic instruction to students. Most institutions' academic year begins in August/September and ends in May/June.

accepted/admitted/admission – a description that is given to a prospective student or applicant that has met the college entrance requirements. Admission types may include but not limited to first-time freshman, transfer, early admit, dual enrolled, conditional

accreditation – a ranking given to an institution based on general standards or requirements of a private agency. The private agencies provide criteria and evaluate the institutions based on general standards.

ACT *(American College Testing)* – exam that measures English, Math, Reading, and Science skills, scores range from 1-36, one of the most common scores required by institutions of higher learning

Advanced Standing Credit – an academic credit completed at another institution or high school. The credit is applied towards graduation completion or used to substitute a required course.

alumni – persons who have met the academic requirements from an institution and graduated.

application/applying to college – a document or process completed by the prospective student to show interest in the institution. Some applications require a fee.

articulation – an agreement between two or more institutions that addresses the policies in transferring academic courses from institutions.

Associate Degree – a degree of a minimum of 60 hours awarded by a two-year institution. Associate degrees consist of an Associate of Arts and Associate of Science degrees. Associate degrees are usually transferred to four-year institutions.

athletic scholarship – awarded based on athletic ability

audit – permission to attend a course without receiving academic credit.

award letter - a letter provided by financial aid at an institution that details the financials that have been given to the student. Award letters are sent to the student after the student completes the Free Application for Federal Student Aid (FAFSA) and admission application.

Bachelor's Degree *(Baccalaureate)* – a certificate of completion that is awarded to an undergraduate student who completes the academic requirements at a four-year institution. The minimum credit hours for a bachelor's degree is 120 hours.

bookstore – a place where books for required courses are stocked and purchased.

Bridge Courses – courses used to prepare students before the start of an academic year.

Business Office/Bursar - office that is responsible for the institution's financial transactions.

catalog – a publication from the institution that defines policies and procedures, academic programs, curricula and course descriptions.

certificate program – course of study that is designed to provide knowledge of a particular skill. Participants receive a certification or certificate of completion. No academic degree is awarded for completing a certificate program.

church scholarship – awarded based on commitment to and involvement in your faith-based organization

class schedule – a list that identifies courses that are being offered during a semester. Class schedules may include the name of the class, location, time, days, number enrolled, professor,

CLEP *(College Level Examination Program)* – an assessment given to students who desire to receive academic credit for a course that was taken prior to admission. Academic credits are based on the required score received.

college – an institution of higher learning that awards degrees and certificates. The term can also be used to identify academic units within an institution such as the College of Business.

college entrance exam – an assessment designed to measure the student's knowledge of general academic areas. Most institutions require completion and achievement of minimal scores (set by the institution) on national exams such as the ACT and SAT prior to admission.

commencement – the act of graduating from the university. Participating in commencement does not guarantee graduation and receipt of a degree.

common application – a general application that is accepted by several institutions and submitted for consideration for admission. Students complete one application and that application is submitted to several institutions.

community scholarship – awarded based on leadership and community service

commuter – a student who lives off campus and takes classes on campus.

Conditional Admit – an admission status that is given to a prospective student who does not meet the general admission standards.

course numbers – a number used to identify a course. A Math course may be identified as Math 204

credit hour – the number of hours assigned to academic courses. Credit hours are measured by the amount of time spent in a course.

curriculum – courses that are needed to complete a program of study. Students should follow their curriculum to receive a certificate or degree.

D

Dean – the leader of an academic unit at an institution. e.g. Dean of Business, Dean of Education.

default – failure to repay a loan or debt.

degree - a reward for successfully completing a program of study.

Doctorate – the highest academic degree awarded by an institution.

double/dual major – students who complete two curricula of study and graduate with two bachelor's degrees.

drop/add – permission that is given to a student to drop and/or add a course. Specific dates are generally given to students before charges are incurred.

dual credit – courses that are counted toward high school and college graduation.

dual enrollment – program that allows high school students to enroll in college courses.

EFC *(Expected Family Contribution)* – the amount determined by federal student aid that is expected from the student to pay towards their education.

elective – a course that is not specifically required by your academic major. Several electives are offered and usually are part of a curriculum.

enrollment – the time during which a student completes registration, selects courses, and satisfies financials at an institution.

extracurricular activities – programs or organizations that are outside of the classroom. Student government, Greek organizations, clubs, recreational, athletics are some extracurricular activities.

FAFSA *(Free Application for Federal Student Aid)* – application to be considered for financial assistance from the federal government. Financial assistance may include: grants, loans, work study or other federal programs.

federal work study – need-based program designed to assist students with paying for their educational expenses while enrolled in college. Students are considered for work study after the completion of the FAFSA .

fee waiver – voucher given to the student to assist with college entrance exams or application fees

fees – additional charges that are not included in your tuition for materials or services which may include mailbox, technology, lab, etc.

final exams – assessment given to students at the end of a semester to determine content mastery of a course. Final exams are scheduled on a date and time determined by either the professor or institution.

financial aid package – letter that outlines the total cost of education at a particular college and the types of funds you'll receive — including federal, state, and school sources.

first-generation – student whose parents have never attended a post-secondary institution

fraternity – a social organization of male students on a college campus, typically named using Greek letters

freshman – first-year student in high school or college

full-time student - a student who is enrolled in the number of hours or courses the school considers to be full-time attendance, typically 12 or more

Geographic region – areas divided in the United States

Connecticut (CT)	Illinois (IL)	Alabama (AL)	Alaska (AK)
Maine (ME)	Indiana (IN)	Arkansas (AR)	Arizona (AZ)
Massachusetts (MA)	Iowa (IA)	Delaware (DE)	California (CA)
New Hampshire (NH)	Kansas (KS)	District of Columbia (DC)	Colorado (CO)
New Jersey (NJ)	Michigan (MI)	Florida (FL)	Hawaii (HI)
New York (NY)	Minnesota (MN)	Georgia (GA)	Idaho (ID)
Pennsylvania (PA)	Missouri (MO)	Kentucky (KY)	Montana (MT)
Rhode Island (RI)	Nebraska (NE)	Louisiana (LA)	Nevada (NV)
Vermont (VT)	North Dakota (ND)	Maryland (MD)	New Mexico (NM)
	Ohio (OH)	Mississippi (MS)	Oregon (OR)
	South Dakota (SD)	North Carolina (NC)	Utah (UT)
	Wisconsin (WI)	Oklahoma (OK)	Washington (WA)
		South Carolina (SC)	Wyoming (WY)
		Tennessee (TN)	
		Texas (TX)	
		Virginia (VA)	
		West Virginia (WV)	

general education – courses that provide basic knowledge of a subject. General education courses are usually completed during freshman and sophomore years.

gifts – money given to the student to pay for college

GPA *(Grade Point Average)* - measurement of a student's accumulated final grades earned in courses. A grade point average (GPA) is calculated by dividing the total amount of grade points earned by the total amount of credit hours attempted and may range from 0.0 to 4.0 or 5.0. Calculation of GPAs may vary by institution.

graduate - a person who has earned a degree or diploma from a school, college, or university.

Graduate degree – degree received after completing a Master, Specialist, or Doctoral academic program

graduation – receipt of a diploma or degree earned from a school, college, or university

grant – student aid based on financial need that does not have to be repaid, typically government-funded

greek – referring to fraternities and sororities

in-state student – one who resides in the state of the school he or she attends

in-state tuition – cost of attending a school for students who reside in the state where the school is located

internship – temporary, unpaid employment for a student that usually teaches skills that are related to your major

junior – third-year student in high school or college who has earned the required number of credits for that classification

lecture – a talk or speech given to a group of people on a particular subject

letter of recommendation – a document in which the writer assesses the qualities, characteristics, and capabilities of an individual's ability to perform a particular task

loan – a form of financial assistance that must be repaid to the lender with interest

major – primary area of study

Master's degree - a degree awarded to graduate students. A master's degree is a degree that can only be earned after a bachelor's

merit-based scholarship – awarded based on academics and talents

mid-terms – assessments that are given during the middle of the semester/quarter to determine mastery of material covered during the first half of the semester

military financial assistance – funds available for students from parent participation in the military

minor – secondary area of study. Fewer classes are required for a minor.

minority scholarship – awarded to smaller groups, typically based on gender or race

need-based – financial assistance that is awarded based on the student's resources to pay for college

non-resident – a student who is not an official resident of the state where a public university is located. Tuition at public universities is more expensive for non-residents.

non-degree - a student who is taking classes but not has not declared a major

office hours – time set aside by professors and teaching assistants for students to visit their offices and ask questions or discuss the course. Hours are typically posted at the beginning of the term denoting when and where students should report.

online classes – courses taken on the computer instead of inside a traditional classroom

orientation – program and activities designed to give students and parents an overview of the school, typically for freshmen and transferring students, and occur the week before school begins

out-of-state student – individual who attends a school outside of the state where he or she resides

out-of-state tuition – fees paid by students who are not residents of the state where they are attending school

part-time student – a student who has not enrolled in enough credit hours to be classified as a full-time student, as defined by your college or university; typically nine hours or less

Pell grant – financial assistance that is need-based and determined by the Federal Government using information provided from the FAFSA

Perkins Loan – need-based, low-interest student loan. No interest is accrued while the student is enrolled at least part-time.

personal statement – short essay written by the student that details characteristics

PIN *(Personal Identification Number)* – a number assigned to allow students to sign their Free Application for Federal Student Aid (FAFSA)

PLUS *(Parent Loan for Undergraduate Student)* - Federal loan available to parents to borrow up to the cost of attendance. The parent is responsible for the interest.

pre-requisite – a class that must be completed before enrollment in another class

private institution - a school that is funded by private sources (i.e. alumni, grants, philanthropists, etc.) and relies heavily on tuition and fees as a source of operation and income

private student loans - loans not issued by the federal government and are available for parents to cover education expenses, usually have a high interest rate

probation – a warning given to students who display poor academic performance

program of study – the major of a degree that a student seeks to earn (e.g. Biology)

promissory note – a legal document signed by the student (or parent) that lists the terms and conditions of a loan and signifies a promise to repay

PSAT/NMSQT *(Preliminary Scholastic Assessment Test/National Merit Scholar Qualifying Test)* - exam that helps students prepare for the SAT and is also used to determine eligibility for the National Merit Scholarship Program. Scores range from 320-1520

public institution – A university that is funded by the government

regular admission - student meets all of the requirements that are necessary to enroll in an institution

resident – a student who lives in and meets the requirements for the state where a college or university is located

SAT Subject Tests – Exams that measure specific subject areas: Math, Science, English, History, and Foreign Languages. Scores range from 200 – 800. Subscores for English range from 20-80.

SAT Test *(Suite of Assessments)* – exam that measures critical reading, math, and writing, scores range from 200–800

school/donor scholarship – awarded from a school or private donor

selective service registration – required for males between the ages of 18 and 25 and must be completed to receive federal aid

semester – academic term that is typically one-half the school year (e.g. Fall semester, Spring semester)

senior – fourth-year high school or college student who has earned the required credits for that classification

sorority - a social organization of female students on a college campus, typically named using Greek letters

sophomore – second-year high school or college student who has earned the required credits for that classification

Stafford Loan – loan for undergraduate students that must be repaid. Government pays the interest and repayment begins 9 months after graduation.

state aid – awarded by the state in which you reside

Student Aid Report (SAR) - summary of the information submitted in the Free Application for Federal Student Aid (FAFSA)

Subsidized Loan – borrowed funding on which the federal government pays interest while the student is in college

terms and conditions - requirements that must be met to secure and/or provide funding

transcript – an official academic record from a specific school that lists courses completed, grades, and attendance information

transfer – a student who withdraws from one school to attend another

undecided – a student who is officially enrolled in college without declaring a major.

Unsubsidized Loan – loan for which the borrower is fully responsible for the interest regardless of the loan status. Interest on unsubsidized loans accrues from the date of disbursement and continues throughout the life of the loan.

work study – type of financial assistance awarded based on need and usually provides a job on campus for the student

Appendix

Just in case you didn't have enough room to explore!

What's included?
- College Entrance Exams *(In case you have more tests to list.)*
- Bonus School
- Top Choice
- Campus Visit Checklist (4)
- Funding Sources *(In case you have more funding to list.)*
- Scholarships *(In case you have more scholarships to list.)*

APPENDIX A — COLLEGE ENTRANCE EXAMS

TEST 1	DATE OF TEST	LOCATION

SCORE	SUBSCORES	
	Subject Area	*Score*

TEST 2	DATE OF TEST	LOCATION

SCORE	SUBSCORES	
	Subject Area	*Score*

TEST 3	DATE OF TEST	LOCATION

SCORE	SUBSCORES	
	Subject Area	*Score*

TEST 4	DATE OF TEST	LOCATION

SCORE	SUBSCORES	
	Subject Area	*Score*

TEST 5		DATE OF TEST	LOCATION
SCORE	SUBSCORES		
	Subject Area		Score

TEST 6		DATE OF TEST	LOCATION
SCORE	SUBSCORES		
	Subject Area		Score

TEST DATES TO REMEMBER

TEST	DATE	COST

APPENDIX B BONUS SCHOOL

82

Research information using the internet and/or library, or find available information in the counseling office at your school. Most information can be located on the school's website

SCHOOL'S NAME

STUDENT POPULATION

DATE SCHEDULED FOR HIGH SCHOOL CAMPUS TOUR(S)

SCHOOL'S MISSION STATEMENT

TYPE OF SCHOOL *(Public/State, Private, Online, Vocational, Technical, Community/Junior)*

TOWN'S POPULATION *(Where the college is located?)*

SCHOOL'S ADDRESS

CITY

STATE

ZIP

DISTANCE FROM HOME *(Use a map search tool to determine the mileage.)*

TRAVEL TIME FROM YOUR HOME TO THE SCHOOL *(Use a map search tool to determine the travel time.)*

AUTOMOBILE	TRAIN	BUS	PLANE

TIME ZONE

SCHOOL'S WEBSITE

PHONE NUMBERS

MAIN CAMPUS	ADMISSION
FINANCIAL AID	**DEPARTMENT YOU ARE INTERESTED IN**

SCHOOL'S SOCIAL MEDIA

(f) _____

(t) _____

(in) _____

(yt) _____

(g+) _____

Other: _____

RELIGIOUS AFFILIATION *(If applicable)*

PREFERRED MAJOR _____

DOES THIS SCHOOL OFFER YOUR PREFERRED MAJOR? Yes ◯ No ◯

IF NO, ARE YOU WILLING TO CHANGE YOUR MAJOR? Yes ◯ No ◯

If no, eliminate this school. If yes, continue.

PREFERRED MINOR _____

Estimated Expenses

	FALL	SPRING	YEARLY TOTAL
TUITION			
In-state			
Out-of-state			
HOUSING			
Single			
Double			
OTHER FEES			
Meal Plan			
Mailbox Rental			
Books/Supplies			
Health Insurance			
Activity Fee			
Technology Fee			
Capital Improvement Fee			
TOTAL EXPENSES			

*Other fees may include: Travel Expenses (associated with traveling to and from campus to your family's place of residence at the start/end of the year and for holidays), etc.

Admission Requirements

SCHOOL REQUIREMENT	SCHOOL AVERAGE	YOURS
GPA		
SAT		
ACT		

AVAILABLE SCHOLARSHIPS

ARE THERE ANY SCHOLARSHIPS AVAILABLE? Yes ◯ No ◯

If so, what is the deadline? _____

ARE THERE ANY ESSAY(S) REQUIRED? Yes ◯ No ◯

If so, what is the deadline? _____

TOPIC 1	TOPIC 2	TOPIC 3

ARE THERE ALTERNATIVE ADMISSION REQUIREMENTS? Yes ◯ No ◯

If so, what are the requirements? _____
_____
_____

(Note: If you are an athlete, check NCAA requirements for incoming freshmen.)

What's next?

Now, it's time to request general information from the school. Fill out a form online on the college website or call the admission office. Determine how long it will take to get the requested information.

DATE REQUESTED _____ **DATE RECEIVED** _____

DOES THIS SCHOOL HAVE MY PREFERRED MAJOR?
Yes ◯ No ◯

DOES THIS SCHOOL HAVE MY PREFERRED MINOR?
Yes ◯ No ◯

IS THIS SCHOOL TOO FAR FROM HOME?
Yes ◯ No ◯

DO I MEET THE STANDARD ADMISSION REQUIREMENTS? Yes ◯ No ◯

IS THERE AN ESSAY REQUIRED?
Yes ◯ No ◯ *If so, what is the topic?*
_____
_____

DO I NEED RECOMMENDATION LETTERS?
Yes ◯ No ◯ *If so, how many and by whom?*
_____
_____

DO MY PARENTS/GUARDIANS APPROVE OF THIS SCHOOL? Yes ◯ No ◯

Final Expense Calculations

TUITION COST	TRAVEL COST
TOTAL ESTIMATED COST PER YEAR	HOUSING APPLICATION FEE

TOTAL YEARLY COST _____ X ____ YEARS TO COMPLETE = _____ TOTAL COST TO COMPLETE DEGREE

DUE DATE FOR PAYMENT *Failure to make payments may affect future enrollments*	PAYMENT PLAN OPTIONS? Yes ◯ No ◯

Funding Sources

Have you completed the Free Application for Federal Student Aid (FAFSA)? Yes ◯ No ◯

SCHOLARSHIPS

SCHOLARSHIP NAME 1	DEADLINE
LETTERS OF RECOMMENDATION	
GPA REQUIREMENTS	OTHER REQUIREMENTS

SCHOLARSHIP NAME 2	DEADLINE
LETTERS OF RECOMMENDATION	
GPA REQUIREMENTS	OTHER REQUIREMENTS

SCHOLARSHIP NAME 3	DEADLINE
LETTERS OF RECOMMENDATION	
GPA REQUIREMENTS	OTHER REQUIREMENTS

SCHOLARSHIP NAME 4	DEADLINE
LETTERS OF RECOMMENDATION	
GPA REQUIREMENTS	OTHER REQUIREMENTS

OTHER TYPES OF FUNDING

Do you have the financial means secured to attend this school? Yes ○ No ○

TYPE OF FUNDING 1

| DATE AWARDED | AMOUNT OF FUNDING | DEADLINE TO SECURE FUNDING |

TERMS & CONDITIONS

TYPE OF FUNDING 2

| DATE AWARDED | AMOUNT OF FUNDING | DEADLINE TO SECURE FUNDING |

TERMS & CONDITIONS

TYPE OF FUNDING 3

| DATE AWARDED | AMOUNT OF FUNDING | DEADLINE TO SECURE FUNDING |

TERMS & CONDITIONS

TYPE OF FUNDING 4

| DATE AWARDED | AMOUNT OF FUNDING | DEADLINE TO SECURE FUNDING |

TERMS & CONDITIONS

TYPE OF FUNDING 5

| DATE AWARDED | AMOUNT OF FUNDING | DEADLINE TO SECURE FUNDING |

TERMS & CONDITIONS

Academics

MAJOR	DEGREE I WILL RECEIVE
How many credit hours will I need to complete a degree?	How many years will it take to complete this degree?
MINOR	DEGREE I WILL RECEIVE
How many credit hours will I need to complete a degree?	How many years will it take to complete this degree?

Admission Requirements

Do you meet the standard admission requirements? Yes ◯ No ◯

If not, are there alternative admission requirements? List alternative admission requirements.
_____
_____
_____

Is early admission available as an option? Yes ◯ No ◯

(Note: You will need your academic transcript to complete the activity below. Request your transcript from your counselor or records clerk.)

CURRENT GPA	REQUIRED GPA FOR GIVEN COLLEGE

INCOMING FRESHMAN ADMISSION REQUIREMENTS

COURSES	REQUIRED CREDIT HOURS	COMPLETED
English		
Math		
Science		
History		
Foreign Language		
Advanced Elective(s)		
Arts		
Technology		
Other		
Other		

Most colleges have course requirements for incoming freshmen. Based on the requirements, look at your transcript and evaluate courses that you have completed. Place a final grade in the box, if you have completed it. Additional spaces are available.

NEED: CURRENT TRANSCRIPT

CURRENT GPA	REQUIRED GPA FOR GIVEN COLLEGE

COURSES	9TH	10TH	11TH	12TH	How many does this college require?
		Check if completed.			
English					
Math					
Science					
History					
Foreign Language					
Advanced Elective(s)					
Fine Arts					
Technology					
Economics					
Physical Education					
Health					
Speech					
Other					
Other					

*Add other course requirements and schedule an appointment with your counselor to discuss any courses or discrepancies that you need to complete high school graduation requirements.

PHONE LOGS FROM SCHOOL

DATE	PHONE NUMBER	PERSON YOU SPOKE TO	COMMENTS

SCHOOL'S CONTACTS

REGISTRAR CONTACTS	TELEPHONE NUMBER

DEPARTMENT CONTACTS	TELEPHONE NUMBER

ADVISOR'S NAME	ADVISOR'S TELEPHONE NUMBER
DATE APPLICATION COMPLETED AND MAILED IN	DATE ADMITTED/ACCEPTED/REJECTED
HAVE YOU COMPLETED THE FAFSA? Yes ◯ No ◯	FINANCIAL AID NUMBER

HAVE YOU APPLIED FOR HOUSING? Yes ◯ No ◯

*If yes, dormitory preferred*_____ *dormitory assigned* _____

FRESHMAN ORIENTATION DATE	NOTES
HAVE YOU MADE YOUR SCHEDULE? Yes ◯ No ◯	HOW MANY CREDIT HOURS ARE YOU TAKING?

CLASSES YOU HAVE REGISTERED FOR

1ST SEMESTER	PROFESSOR

PHONE LOGS FROM SCHOOL

DATE	PHONE NUMBER	PERSON YOU SPOKE TO	COMMENTS

Important Deadlines

Include deadlines for admissions, scholarships, financial aid, campus tours, college entrance exams, auditions, high school class days and other important dates.

EVENT	DATE OF EVENT	DEADLINE TO APPLY

APPLICATION DEADLINE	_____
APPLICATION FEE	_____
DATE APPLIED	_____
DATE ACCEPTED	_____
DATE DENIED	_____

ALTERNATIVE ADMISSION REQUIREMENTS

_____

_____

_____

Notes

APPENDIX C — COLLEGE 1

Campus Visit

Before

- ○ Contact the school
- ○ Pick a Date (Preferably Monday – Thursday) Best Times: Spring of Junior year or Early September. *(Check school holiday breaks)*
- ○ Get a contact name
- ○ Have directions to the location of the tour
- ○ Contact departments that may not be included in the tour
- ○ Be familiar with the school by exploring its website
- ○ Get a map of the campus

During

- ○ Have questions ready for tour guide, students, faculty and staff
- ○ Visit the cafeteria, a dorm room, admissions, financial aid, departments *(Schedule prior to visiting)*
- ○ Get pamphlets/brochures/school newspaper
- ○ Take notes/pictures
- ○ Talk to students who are enrolled

After

- ○ Follow up with any additional questions and thank-you letters via email or mail
- ○ Review your notes
- ○ Decide if you are less or more interested
- ○ Compile your notes and look at things you liked versus things you don't

Visit Information

COLLEGE NAME	DATE OF VISIT
TOUR GUIDE	RECRUITER

POSSIBLE DATES TO VISIT/ RESERVED FOR HIGH SCHOOL STUDENTS		

Questions

For Students
1.
2.
3.

For Staff
1.
2.
3.

For Faculty
1.
2.
3.

Rate Your Experince

CAMPUS
○ Excellent ○ Very Good ○ Good ○ Not Bad ○ Bad

TOUR GUIDE
○ Excellent ○ Very Good ○ Good ○ Not Bad ○ Bad

STUDENT LIFE
○ Excellent ○ Very Good ○ Good ○ Not Bad ○ Bad

DORMS
○ Excellent ○ Very Good ○ Good ○ Not Bad ○ Bad

HOUSING
○ Excellent ○ Very Good ○ Good ○ Not Bad ○ Bad

ACADEMICS
○ Excellent ○ Very Good ○ Good ○ Not Bad ○ Bad

CAFETERIA
○ Excellent ○ Very Good ○ Good ○ Not Bad ○ Bad

MET EXPECTATIONS
○ Excellent ○ Very Good ○ Good ○ Not Bad ○ Bad

Important Contacts

	NAME	NUMBER
Admissions		
Financial Aid		
Housing		
Academic Department		
Food Services (Meal Plan)		
Coaches (If an Athlete)		
Other		
Other		
Other		
Other		

Notes

___
___
___
___
___
___
___
___
___
___
___
___
___
___
___
___
___

C COLLEGE 2

Campus Visit

Before

- ○ Contact the school
- ○ Pick a Date (Preferably Monday – Thursday) Best Times: Spring of Junior year or Early September. *(Check school holiday breaks)*
- ○ Get a contact name
- ○ Have directions to the location of the tour
- ○ Contact departments that may not be included in the tour
- ○ Be familiar with the school by exploring its website
- ○ Get a map of the campus

During

- ○ Have questions ready for tour guide, students, faculty and staff
- ○ Visit the cafeteria, a dorm room, admissions, financial aid, departments *(Schedule prior to visiting)*
- ○ Get pamphlets/brochures/school newspaper
- ○ Take notes/pictures
- ○ Talk to students who are enrolled

After

- ○ Follow up with any additional questions and thank-you letters via email or mail
- ○ Review your notes
- ○ Decide if you are less or more interested
- ○ Compile your notes and look at things you liked versus things you don't

Visit Information

COLLEGE NAME	DATE OF VISIT
TOUR GUIDE	RECRUITER

POSSIBLE DATES TO VISIT/ RESERVED FOR HIGH SCHOOL STUDENTS

Questions

For Students
1.
2.
3.

For Staff
1.
2.
3.

For Faculty
1.
2.
3.

Rate Your Experince

CAMPUS
○ Excellent ○ Very Good ○ Good ○ Not Bad ○ Bad

TOUR GUIDE
○ Excellent ○ Very Good ○ Good ○ Not Bad ○ Bad

STUDENT LIFE
○ Excellent ○ Very Good ○ Good ○ Not Bad ○ Bad

DORMS
○ Excellent ○ Very Good ○ Good ○ Not Bad ○ Bad

HOUSING
○ Excellent ○ Very Good ○ Good ○ Not Bad ○ Bad

ACADEMICS
○ Excellent ○ Very Good ○ Good ○ Not Bad ○ Bad

CAFETERIA
○ Excellent ○ Very Good ○ Good ○ Not Bad ○ Bad

MET EXPECTATIONS
○ Excellent ○ Very Good ○ Good ○ Not Bad ○ Bad

Important Contacts

	NAME	NUMBER
Admissions		
Financial Aid		
Housing		
Academic Department		
Food Services (Meal Plan)		
Coaches (If an Athlete)		
Other		
Other		
Other		
Other		

Notes

C COLLEGE 3

Campus Visit

Before

- ○ Contact the school
- ○ Pick a Date (Preferably Monday –Thursday) Best Times: Spring of Junior year or Early September. *(Check school holiday breaks)*
- ○ Get a contact name
- ○ Have directions to the location of the tour
- ○ Contact departments that may not be included in the tour
- ○ Be familiar with the school by exploring its website
- ○ Get a map of the campus

During

- ○ Have questions ready for tour guide, students, faculty and staff
- ○ Visit the cafeteria, a dorm room, admissions, financial aid, departments *(Schedule prior to visiting)*
- ○ Get pamphlets/brochures/school newspaper
- ○ Take notes/pictures
- ○ Talk to students who are enrolled

After

- ○ Follow up with any additional questions and thank-you letters via email or mail
- ○ Review your notes
- ○ Decide if you are less or more interested
- ○ Compile your notes and look at things you liked versus things you don't

Visit Information

COLLEGE NAME	DATE OF VISIT
TOUR GUIDE	RECRUITER

POSSIBLE DATES TO VISIT/ RESERVED FOR HIGH SCHOOL STUDENTS

Questions

For Students
1.
2.
3.

For Staff
1.
2.
3.

For Faculty
1.
2.
3.

Rate Your Experince

CAMPUS
○ Excellent ○ Very Good ○ Good ○ Not Bad ○ Bad

TOUR GUIDE
○ Excellent ○ Very Good ○ Good ○ Not Bad ○ Bad

STUDENT LIFE
○ Excellent ○ Very Good ○ Good ○ Not Bad ○ Bad

DORMS
○ Excellent ○ Very Good ○ Good ○ Not Bad ○ Bad

HOUSING
○ Excellent ○ Very Good ○ Good ○ Not Bad ○ Bad

ACADEMICS
○ Excellent ○ Very Good ○ Good ○ Not Bad ○ Bad

CAFETERIA
○ Excellent ○ Very Good ○ Good ○ Not Bad ○ Bad

MET EXPECTATIONS
○ Excellent ○ Very Good ○ Good ○ Not Bad ○ Bad

Important Contacts

	NAME	NUMBER
Admissions		
Financial Aid		
Housing		
Academic Department		
Food Services (Meal Plan)		
Coaches (If an Athlete)		
Other		
Other		
Other		
Other		

Notes

APPENDIX D FUNDING SOURCES

TYPE OF FUNDING 1

DATE AWARDED	AMOUNT OF FUNDING	DEADLINE TO SECURE FUNDING

TERMS & CONDITIONS

TYPE OF FUNDING 2

DATE AWARDED	AMOUNT OF FUNDING	DEADLINE TO SECURE FUNDING

TERMS & CONDITIONS

TYPE OF FUNDING 3

DATE AWARDED	AMOUNT OF FUNDING	DEADLINE TO SECURE FUNDING

TERMS & CONDITIONS

TYPE OF FUNDING 4

DATE AWARDED	AMOUNT OF FUNDING	DEADLINE TO SECURE FUNDING

TERMS & CONDITIONS

TYPE OF FUNDING 5

DATE AWARDED	AMOUNT OF FUNDING	DEADLINE TO SECURE FUNDING

TERMS & CONDITIONS

TYPE OF FUNDING 6

DATE AWARDED	AMOUNT OF FUNDING	DEADLINE TO SECURE FUNDING

TERMS & CONDITIONS

TYPE OF FUNDING 7

DATE AWARDED	AMOUNT OF FUNDING	DEADLINE TO SECURE FUNDING

TERMS & CONDITIONS

TYPE OF FUNDING 8

DATE AWARDED	AMOUNT OF FUNDING	DEADLINE TO SECURE FUNDING

TERMS & CONDITIONS

TYPE OF FUNDING 9

DATE AWARDED	AMOUNT OF FUNDING	DEADLINE TO SECURE FUNDING

TERMS & CONDITIONS

TYPE OF FUNDING 10

DATE AWARDED	AMOUNT OF FUNDING	DEADLINE TO SECURE FUNDING

TERMS & CONDITIONS

APPENDIX E — SCHOLARSHIPS

SCHOLARSHIP NAME 1	DEADLINE
LETTERS OF RECOMMENDATION	
GPA REQUIREMENTS	**OTHER REQUIREMENTS**

SCHOLARSHIP NAME 2	DEADLINE
LETTERS OF RECOMMENDATION	
GPA REQUIREMENTS	**OTHER REQUIREMENTS**

SCHOLARSHIP NAME 3	DEADLINE
LETTERS OF RECOMMENDATION	
GPA REQUIREMENTS	**OTHER REQUIREMENTS**

SCHOLARSHIP NAME 4	DEADLINE
LETTERS OF RECOMMENDATION	
GPA REQUIREMENTS	**OTHER REQUIREMENTS**

SCHOLARSHIP NAME 5	DEADLINE
LETTERS OF RECOMMENDATION	
GPA REQUIREMENTS	**OTHER REQUIREMENTS**

SCHOLARSHIP NAME 6	DEADLINE
LETTERS OF RECOMMENDATION	
GPA REQUIREMENTS	**OTHER REQUIREMENTS**

RESOURCES

AMERICAN COLLEGE TESTING
http://www.act.org/

BIG FUTURE BY THE COLLEGE BOARD
https://bigfuture.collegeboard.org/

CAPPEX
https://www.cappex.com/

COLLEGE BOARD
https://www.collegeboard.org/

FEDERAL STUDENT AID: AN OFFICE OF THE U.S. DEPARTMENT OF EDUCATION
https://fafsa.ed.gov/

FASTWEB
http://www.fastweb.com/

MERRIAM-WEBSTER COLLEGIATE DICTIONARY
http://www.merriam-webster.com/

NICHE
https://colleges.niche.com/

PETERSONS
https://www.petersons.com/

UNIGO
https://www.unigo.com/

UNIVERSITY LANGUAGES SERVICES
https://www.universitylanguage.com/

U.S. DEPARTMENT OF EDUCATION
http://www.ed.gov/

About the Author

Andrea Jones-Davis

Andrea Jones-Davis is a native of Grenada, Mississippi who has devoted her life to educating others. She holds a Bachelor of Business in Marketing and Public Management and Leadership Certificate from Jackson State University and a Master of Teaching Arts and Educational Specialist in Educational Leadership from Mississippi College.

While employed as a classroom teacher and Instructional Technology Facilitator, Andrea honed her education and training skills and later founded a mobile learning lab, Toot, Teach & Roll, which provides unique experiences for learners of all ages. Additionally, she was a participant in Leadership Greater Jackson's Class of 2012 and recognized as one of Mississippi Business Journal's Top 40 Under 40.

Andrea's work as an Assistant Director of Undergraduate Recruitment strengthened her desire to develop a program that caters to college preparedness. But it was her work with children in the community and guiding her son and-most recently-her daughter-in preparing for college entry that sparked the brainchild that is now The Next Chapter. Andrea believes in lifelong learning and wants to assist other prospective high school graduates in preparing for one of life's greatest milestones by planning for and choosing the school of higher education most suited to their needs.

Currently, Andrea is Executive Director of JSUOnline and works hard to ensure that those who want to learn have access to and exercise their options. However, she makes sure to maintain a great life-work balance by cultivating her creativity through journaling and arts and crafts, listening to music, and spending time with family and friends. In addition to these notable accomplishments, Andrea has obtained certifications as a Google™ Educator and Smartboard™ Trainer.

www.ingramcontent.com/pod-product-compliance
Lightning Source LLC
Chambersburg PA
CBHW081210170426
43198CB00018B/2915